Darkside of the Moon

Melissa Rivera

Presentation by *BookLeaf Publishing*

Web: www.bookleafpub.com

E-mail: info@bookleafpub.com

ISBN: 9789357613712

First edition 2022

This book is dedicated to all the souls searching for a reason. The truth is nothing in life has purpose without you.

ACKNOWLEDGEMENT

Thank you to all my amazing supporters for always believing in me. Most importantly though, thank you to my mother for teaching me to see the light through all my darkest situations.

A huge thank you goes out to Devon Elliot who helped me shape these thoughts into something more.

Battlefield

His tears, my tears, our tears.
Frustrations thanks to miscommunication.
He just wants to color the world bright yellow.
I just want to wipe the slate clean.

Her tears, my tears, our tears.
Desperation for clear communication.
She just wants to make me smile.
I just want peace and quiet.

To them the world is so big and wondrous.
To me the world is slowly closing in.
To them I am so strong, and magical.
To me I am so tired, and dull.

His eyes, my eyes, our eyes.
We see the world so differently.
Her eyes, my eyes, our eyes.
We see the world so distinctly.

Some days I feel like I'm failing,
But then I take the time to look through
The eyes of a child and,
I know we will be okay.

Coronation Day

If you ever cross my path again, it will be the
last time you see me.
If you ever try to cross me, know it will be the
last time you're scheming.
If you try to cross the waves with my family
know I will drown you in your pathetic sorrows.

You want to hold as much power as I, but you
and I know you pick on people half your size.
A battle with me is something you can't surmise.
A battle with me would be your last! That's why
you run knowing I'll kick that a–

You run to the dream world hoping that I can't
keep up.
Well, you're not the only master of not giving a
f—-
I can astral project too.

Use that imagination we both know what I
would do.
That's why you make sure every fight is out of
the public view.

Once I place that crown on my head you fear
that everyone would treat you as if you were
dead.
That is a fate I agree you deserve, because you
have some nerve with the values you hold.

Your vision would be out of orbit, your head
would be bobbed into the waters.
You think this would be your baptism but
instead this is the last time you're swimming.
Some may think these thoughts are too dark.
They wonder how true my words actually are.

Have no fear this was all just a dream, but
should she come clean, just know every word,
every spell casted is as real as your ex who
never lasted.

Hope

Hope is like…

Hope is…

What is hope?

I hate that word…

There is no H O P E.
Read that in an obnoxious voice.

F U C K hope.
I never hoped for anything in my life.
That's a lie.

I manifest.

Manifest your dreams, and wishes.
Hope never brought me anything but broken
pieces.

Like I hoped my dad wasn't guilty that day
when my heart broke,
Like I hoped my best friend wouldn't turn
against me over money, or coke.

I hoped my family would stop being cruel one
day, but one day came & I saw even more pain.

No, I manifest.
I manifest what you see before me.
I create my reality.

New car, that's me.
New apartment, that's me.
Whole new job, THAT'S ME.

Hope has not a thing for me.
If we speak on faith….now faith is a different
topic, but don't ever ask me .
Hope is not worth the heartbreak it causes.

Crystal Ball

Should you stay in the empty space while
everyone goes,
you will never see past those tall empty walls.
Your voice will echo with each breath you take,
if you stay while everyone goes.

You should know when to walk away.
You should know when it's time to move on.
These empty spaces are not your home.
We are travelers, we go where we are called.

You should know when to leave it all behind.
Don't hang out, you'll start to feel confined.
These empty spaces still have a home.
For some reason my heart calls to them in the
middle of the night.

These empty spaces I can't seem to let them go..
Even though no one seems to be home.
I tell everyone it's time to flee,
while on the inside it really is destroying me.

It hurts to walk away, but I must.
These empty spaces are not something you can
trust.

Should you stay in the empty voids,
Your past is what the future holds.

Stars in the Sky

I'm GUILTY.
I'm guilty of being a human.

I have so many dark little pleasures.
I know I shouldn't.

I'm a leader.
Don't follow me, I'm lost.

I'm as maaad as everrr.
I have guilty pleasures.

I love money, though I shouldn't.
Release material items into the earthly realms.
You can not touch heaven as a spiritual leader if
you lust for a life of luxury..
You're not elevated if you like low vibrational
foundations.
How dare you claim to lead but then ask to be
paid.
Your services should be free.
These are all things that have been said to me.

I can't help it. I'm just guilty.
It must be the Taurus in me.

Call me MR. KRABS because I love me some
Money
Money
Money.

I'm GUILTY!
OH god.
Sue me.

I have dark little pleasures.
I know I shouldn't.

Hey everyone, don't follow the leader!
I'm as mad as ever.
I have guilty pleasures.

I love to see my enemies crash.
I love to see them burn,
am I wrong for taking pride when I send out my
evil eyes?

I don't ever swing first.
I try to play fair.
Why would you try me though?
It will always end in your despair…

That's evil! You shouldn't wish bad on other
people.
Don't you know that there is the law of 3.

Anything you send out comes back to thee x3
So mote it be…

Ugh I can't help it. Even that was a curse.
Stop sending me hexes thinking I won't reverse.
I will send it all back and tether it to an event.
Something you don't know about because you're
not an alchemist.

It does make me happy when you're in pain, but
I don't feel bad
Because you only have yourself to blame.
I have no regrets so they persecute my name.
I can't help it, it must be the Scorpio in me.

What people seem to forget is I am more than
just one person, place, or time.
The theory is that the stars composed me.
I have stardust in my soul, I shine even when it's
dark.
I am not only kind, caring and empathetic.

There is more to me.
I know I'm guilty.
I know I have caused pain.
I am karma in my own way.

I play all the parts I'm meant to play.
I am darkness and I am light.

I am Leo. I shine so bright.

I am a Virgo. I am strategic.
I am Gemini, my cerebral sways me,
like dirty dancing with Patrick Swayze.
Good or bad it doesn't matter. I see two sides to
the coin.
Gemini's are known to have two faces, two
bodies, two souls.

If you stopped to think then you would know,
Gemini's use the information they learned to
move forward in their goals.
They are not two faced, they learned something
new, maybe they heard something…about YOU.

You see because I may be guilty, but you are too.
Every leader has something to say about the way
I conduct my services;
 on display.

The truth is in this game of chess it isn't who is
playing the BEST.
It isn't the one with the purest soul, it isn't the
one who lost control.

The person who wins, is the person who
stopped…
playing the game because…

with mirroring moves you would never win.
We are all part of the universe therefore we
should all know
Our guilty pleasures are nothing to scold.

We are perfect, we are divine.
You can be a leader and still be aligned.
You can love money and still be a guide.
You can love darkness but still be a star in the
sky.

Ella quiere Sonar

Perhaps one day I'll have my life together.
Maybe one day I'll be that person that wakes up
at 4am straps on sneakers,
and greets the morning with a dedicated jog.
I'd come home, get in my waterfall shower that I
dreamed of for years.
I'd pull out a gorgeous outfit from my walk-in
closet with 360 mirrors.
I'd do my hair the way I see these beautiful
women online do their hair, not a piece out of
place.
I'd take my time with my skin routine, and even
dress up my face with the final touches of
makeup that has the same price as my entire
ensemble.

If I had my life together my house would look
straight out of a magazine.
My kitchen would be my safe haven, pools of
sky blue on the walls,
adorned with emerald green, healthy, thriving
plants.
My dishes would always be clean and organized,
cups along the wall,

placed in the coffee corner I decorated so
thoughtfully.
I would never have to hunt for a mug in the
morning, my teas would be
easily accessible, and there would be at least 20+
different flavors to choose from.
There would be honey always available.

One day I'll have my life together!
All the food in my house will be organic.
Everything would be the best of the best.
My neighbors would be so proud to know.
I would have home cooked meals every night
with the freshest ingredients.
You would never see me bringing in boxes full
of children's happiness in the
shape of chicken nuggets.
 No! Every meal would be hand crafted by me.

Perhaps one day I'll have my life together..
But the truth is I don't.
I HATE 4am. Let me sleep.
I HATE running even if the sneakers perfectly
match my workout outfit I got off Amazon.

My life isn't "together".
My shower is not a waterfall, but I love its
warmth on the toughest days.
My closet is small, you can not walk in it.

My mirror is a seven dollar body length mirror
from Walmart that my children are intent on
destroying.
My hair is ALWAYS out of place..
Skincare routine? HA I do a face mask once a
week and call it a day.
Makeup? My arsenal consists of things my
mother bought me for christmas last year,
yes it's expired, don't judge me.

My life is a chaotic mess, not well put together.
You'd never see my life in a magazine..or
Maybe you would as a warning.
What not to do.

My kitchen is always in shambles, dishes full to
the brim no matter
How many rounds I fight.
The trash is always somehow ready to explode.
My plants are crispy from the weeks I just don't
remember their presence.
The coffee corner I tried to create is a keurig
machine and nothing more.
My teas are abundant, at least that's something I
could say..
But they are NOT organized, and my honey is
always running low.
My honey is not aesthetically pleasing or
organic.

I drizzle it anyway.

My life is NOT together.
The food is always junk!
I try my best to cook organically, but have you
seen the prices?!
Guess what children? We're eating Ramen.
Oh snap, the time passed me by.
I guess that's what makes the Golden arches so
rich in color.
Moms like me don't have time to cook.
Small red boxes, bring smiles to their faces, and
mine.
My life is a whirlwind, but at least my children
are fed and happy.
Oh and did I mention my neighbors hate me?
I guess I'm not the perfect stepford wife.

Perhaps one day I'll have my life together…
Or maybe I'll just fall in love with my chaos.
My life is a masterpiece, and everything is as it
should be.

Ghost

Some days I just want to give in.
Day in, day out,
I wait patiently for peace.
I just want to disappear.
I want the privacy that always seems to elude
me.
 It slips through my fingers like the pages in a
book.
The faster I turn the page grasping at every
word, the more I comprehend
the impossible nature of my life.
My life is like A series of Unfortunate Events,
one thing after the next.
I find myself waiting to see how the series ends.
Some days I just wonder what it would be like to
be a ghost.
To feel so weightless I could levitate.
No sense of purpose anchoring me to this
desperate plane.
I would soar into the winds and just let them
capture me.
Drifting into the peaceful feeling of freedom.
If I were a ghost I would dance in the branches
of a weeping willow tree.

Finally feeling one with the universe that gave
me life.
How ironic it must be that in order to understand
existence , one must lose it.
There's something magical about being able to
sweep away the everlasting heaviness of the
burdens of this world.
I am merely a soul having a human experience.

Honeycomb

Busy as a bee, but they don't see me.
Wings fluttering, from one flower to the next.
Worker bee, worker bee, but still they don't see.
Lilies guide the way with their scent so
perplexed.
I'm waiting for the moment where I glow in the
sun.
Busy bee, I want to feel the sunrays caressing
me.
I want to blow in the cool breeze,
Root down into the green.
What it would feel like to be grounded, yet so
free.
Worker bee, worker bee, no I am not a queen.
I was not born with honey.
So for now I must make the money.

Lesson 1

I have lost myself,
Or so it seems.
I have gone so deep that even my own mother
doesn't recognize me.

She is questioning me & all my beliefs.
How could you not trust in me?
Don't you know I'm the only person on this
planet you could trust?

I don't know that because I have felt so alone.
Pitch black, just like the night.
Cold as the darkest winter day.
My heart is closed.
This is the only way.

If you wake me up inside I might just cry.
I don't know who to trust,
All I ask myself is why?

Are you the next person to stab me in my chest?
Did you expect me to say back?
No, because it's always been to my face.

The people I loved the most are the reason for
this break.
My heart pools out every ounce of hatred I once
had.
Fool me once shame on you, fool me twice &
well trust me
There won't be a thrice.

Trust is not something I am capable of.
Can't you see that I am earth's creation?
Mother Gaia embraced me in her loving arms,
while
This infestation that walks her curves destroyed
me.

I am love.
But no, I will not trust.
Steps onto the concrete of mother earth's crust.
Each crack is a reminder that humans destroy
what feeds them life.

I am a child of the night,
I lurk in the shadows and to see the light.
I see the dark and I feel right at home.
Loneliness is something I've always known.

Sirens

My heart feels like a thunderstorm.
Excitement and fear all at once.
Was it fear, or did I just sense all your lies?

Butterflies danced in my eyes, while I
I felt storm winds rip apart their wings.
They steered me away when I got too close.
Yelling "Caution storm approaching!"

Lightning bolted———-------
My heart never skipped a beat.
All I felt was electricity.
How is it that you're lighting up the darkest
parts of me?
You make me so angry.

 Raging tides paced inside my mind.
I was always on the search, but there was
something I could never find.
Wave after wave crushed me when we didn't
speak.
Silence echoed louder than the rain.
Each pebble, each seashell a reminder of wishes
never fulfilled..

How can you pull me in so close when I told you
no?
I'll push you into the krakens den before I ever
let it drown me.
Even worse than your silence… was the fog you
caused.
My mind was playing tricks on me, is that a
shark I see?
Oh no wait, that was just another tale cast from
your thunderous mouth, into the sea.

Did you ever feel the electricity or was it always
just me?

The Audacity

I am free. I am free.
I am free of all your inconsistencies.
I am free of loving you flaws and all.
I freed myself of your eternal grasp.

You drove my mind into the depths unknown.
I was enchanted, but now I know.
You have fallen and I have rose.

You thought you had me, but I saw my way out.
I saw the tunnel and ran towards the light.
Anywhere away from you is where I took flight.
I thought you cared for me, what a mistake I see.

Isn't it a blessing that I am now free..

Toxic Positivity

Marie Antoinette

Mistake after mistake!
Just give me a break.
No break? Oh okay, then I just might bend until
I…
BREAK.
Make the ground shake with every nerve that
aches!
Oh you want to be next to me?
Better tread carefully.
SCREAM.
No, I'm not your dream!
More like your nightmare.
I'll give you goosebumps with every stare.
GLARE.
Truth or dare?
I'll make the choice for you.
Truth is I wish I didn't know you..
Now I dare you to face all that I feel.
I might just SCREAM "let them eat cake!"
Before my unofficial heart…
BREAKS…

Twin Flames

It's been a hell of a year thank god we made it
out.
Tell me all the things you see in me.

When I'm alone I think of you.
You really, really hurt me, it was as if my
sadness made you complete.
I could be myself around you; those were my
beliefs.

Until I started realizing the way you treated me.
I told you all my trials and tribulations, you
became one of them.

I got the chills every time I felt your touch.
You brought out feelings in me I never showed
before.

People were hating us, something we already
knew.
I wanted this bad romance, I didn't want to just
be friends.

Love the Skin I'm in

Thick skin for the win. I don't think I should need thick skin to survive, but I am your creation. If you look at me and you hate what you see, remember you created me. I am all the words you wrapped around that I use as armor. Each layer is a new edition to my exoskeleton. Next time you try to jab me and pierce that needle of a tongue into my veins, be ready to exclaim "Wow, you have thick skin!" I'll smile to your face because not a skin cell will be out of place. You should be aware that "sticks and stones may break my bones, but your words will never hurt me."

Home

Home is where dance battles begin;
Karaoke is blasted.

Home is smudged with sage,
sprinkled in blessed salt, decorated with
powerful crystals at the doors.

Home is where my ancestors roam;
Altar over the front door, may only family enter.

Home is my sacred space, where my children
warm themselves with the love that bounces
from room to room.

Home is where blessings happen.
Home is where the magic happens.

The fortune teller

Dear Crystal Ball,

I'm looking for some clarity. You see, I never thought that all these things would happen to me.

I never thought all these decisions would be up to me. I woke up one day, and I wasn't a kid. I had to learn all the things that make you grown. I think back a lot, like "if I had only known." I took so much for granted. If I could go back I wouldn't do it all the same. Crystal ball I would be more grateful, and take things slow. I would teach myself to heal before my world implodes. I know that I can not change the past, I know it is what it is, and I should just laugh, but Crystal Ball sometimes I just wonder. Why things are the way they are, and how my life became such a huge blunder. I should have seen all the warning signs that screamed out to me. Crystal Ball! I just need clarity. Can you just explain to me?! If I'm not the problem, and I'm doing all my healing, why is it me who is ending up the only one steering? There is nobody else on this boat. It's only me that keeps it afloat. I can feel this ship is sinking. Water is flooding the engines, the sirens are singing. Crystal Ball it's the future you see, where are these seas bringing me? Why endure all these rocky waters, each wave just hits me harder, and harder.

411

Fear is nothing, but an obstacle.
Cross over and be the fool.
Don't stay as the hanged man, or you may miss
your opportunity.

You are the star, be in the spotlight, and radiate.
Take the death card and end the connection with
those who can't stand to share the stage.
This story isn't only about them, they are afraid.
Fear is their obstacle.

Don't be fearful of that tower.
The building was never stable, check out what
was under.
You just might find the Ace of cups, as long as
you don't allow, for the devil
To show up.

Fear is his advocate; he loves to be around it.
Most people allow for this emotion to control
them;
Never looking at the mirror and seeing what
they have become.

Emperor's in reverse because they can't seem to
lead.
We're looking for the Empress please don't be
deceived.
We need someone who can guide the way.
Her intuition listens to the hermit in the wind.

Hearing all the wisdom it whispers.
Passed along by the hierophant, who was ready
to be heard.
Fear aside will bring you the Ace of pentacles.
Each word of advice is made of gold.

Fear will keep you from connecting with the
world.
It's your world, so never allow judgment
clouded by fear to
Spin your wheel of fortune.
The lovers are ready to greet your chariot the
minute you step outside the garden Eve.

Wait until you see that once fear disappears,
you'll learn that
Lillith gifted us with the Ace of Swords to set us
free.
She gave us strength to walk away from men.
Lilith gave us the key to open the doors of
eternity.

Like the moon if you had no fears, you could
control the tides,
High priestess.
Give yourself the justice you deserve.
Remove that fear from your heart. It's absurd.

Reach out and take hold of the Ace of wands.
Bring temperance to your home become the
magican.
An alchemist that takes any remittance, and
somehow turns into a blessing.
Like the Sun your bravery will blind the world.

Fear seems to be the only emotion they know.
Most humans walk the earth with the three of
swords in their heart.
Never, forgiving, or forgetting, puppets that are
afraid of the dark.
Fear is an illusion, don't you ever forget it.

Pearls

Something silver but never gold.
He gave me diamonds for the secrets I hold.
Pearls were gifted for secrets untold.
Something silver but never gold.

Take my heart, please don't break it.
He made me his wife,
but then one night,
he gave me his knife.
He forced me into a fight.
Yelling "HARDER HARDER!"
I was scared I thought,
"Here's my knight…where was his valor?"

His eyes turned red and soon he said,
"I only want to be your man & if I can't have
you no one can!"
Something silver but never gold.
Here lie all the secrets I withhold.

Pearls fell onto the floor.
I screamed "THAT'S IT! NOT A SECOND
MORE!
I'M DONE! LET ME GO! TIME TO STOP
PUTTING ON A SHOW!

UNHAND ME YOU MONSTER IN GUISE!
Can't you see all the tears in my eyes?
You look like a dragon; I'll slay you myself."

Something silver but never gold.
My knight was the villain, I wanted to fold.
I had to save myself. No hero came, so I freed
the kingdom.
I'll never let that dragon back in.

My body's a temple or so I was told…
My castle was finally home and I realized..
I was ALWAYS the gold.
All of my secrets turned into pearls…
& that's part 1 of how I found my worth.

www.ingramcontent.com/pod-product-compliance
Lightning Source LLC
LaVergne TN
LVHW010926200726
843509LV00013B/2103